CW01455311

EMBRACING
22Q

A HELPFUL BOOK FOR PARENTS

WHAT YOU WILL FIND IN THIS BOOK!

Part 1- Understanding this new diagnosis of 22Q includes:
- What is it, how did it happen?
- Who does it affect?
- Medical terms you might hear

Part 2- Health, Growth & Thriving through 22Q
- Common health issues, and how to get through them

Part 3- Family, School & Social Life:
- Parenting 22Q children from birth, to adolescence, and into adulthood.

Part 4- Support Networks and Charities for 22Q.
- List of support groups, charities and benefits to help with you or your child's 22Q journey.

BONUS PAGES! - At the back i have popped in some self care guides, medical team notes and achievement pages for your children's milestones! These really helped me on my journey so i really hope they help you too!

Katy x

TAKE CARE
— of —
YOURSELF

GREAT
THINGS
NEVER COME
from COMFORT
zone

BE KIND
to yourself

you are
INCREDIBLE

You
GOT
this

you
can
DO
hard
things

Welcome to the 22Q Family!
"A Journey of Love, Hope, and Strength"

Hi! My name is Katy, i am a mother of 3 boys, 10, 6 and 3. When my youngest son was born, I thought I knew what to expect.

I had imagined the first cuddles, the milestones, and the future we would build together. But nothing could have prepared me for the moment we were told he had 22q11.2 deletion syndrome.

It was a diagnosis I had never heard of before, and in that instant, our world shifted.

The words from the doctors felt heavy—genetic condition, possible complications, medical needs. My heart ached with fear for his future. Would he be okay? Would he have a good life? How would we explain this to his siblings?

It felt like stepping into an unknown world without a map.

At just one year old, he had open-heart surgery, a moment that no parent is ever truly ready for. The sight of my tiny child in a hospital bed, hooked up to machines, was a pain I can't fully describe. And now, as he approaches another surgery—to help him with his speech—it's a reminder of the journey we are still on.

But here's the part I never expected: as time passed, as my little boy grew into a three-year-old full of laughter, curiosity, and mischief, the worry that once consumed me began to fade. Yes, the challenges are real. Yes, the road is different. But it is also filled with joy, resilience, and an incredible kind of love.

I've learned to celebrate things I once took for granted—the first steps that came a little later but felt like a victory, the first words that were spoken with immense effort but filled my heart with pride. This journey has taught me patience, gratitude, and a deep appreciation for the little things that others might overlook.

One day, my son's doctor said something that stuck with me: *"He is perfect the way he is—he just has some added extras."* That's exactly how I see him now. Not as a diagnosis, but as an incredible little boy who brings light into our lives every single day - and with some added sprinkles!

This book is for you—the parent who has just heard the words "22Q deletion" for the first time. I am here to offer comfort, guidance, and hope. I want you to know that while the journey ahead may not be the one you expected, it is still a beautiful one. There will be challenges, yes—but there will also be moments of pure joy, incredible progress, and an unbreakable bond with your child.

There is help, support, and a community of parents who have walked this path before you. But most importantly, there is hope.

You are not alone.

With warmth and understanding,

Katy & Jett - Mum and Son

Part 1: Understanding 22Q11.2 Deletion Syndrome

What Is 22Q?

If you're reading this, there's a good chance that you, your child, or someone you love has just been diagnosed with 22q11.2 deletion syndrome. First of all, let me start by saying this: take a deep breath.

I know exactly how you feel right now. I remember sitting in a doctor's office, being handed a diagnosis I had never heard of before. Words like "genetic deletion," "chromosomal disorder," and "multi-system condition" were thrown around, and I felt like I had just stepped into a medical textbook I never asked to read. My mind was racing with questions. What does this mean? Will my child be okay? What does the future look like?

If that's where you are right now, I want you to know that it's going to be okay. Yes, this diagnosis is important, but it does not change who your child is. Your baby, your toddler, your growing child—they are still the same wonderful person you love. They just have a few extra challenges, and thankfully, there is a world of medical care, therapies, and support available to help them thrive. So, let's start by breaking things down into something much less scary.

What Exactly Is 22Q?

You might have heard your doctor refer to 22q11.2 deletion syndrome, but it can also be called DiGeorge Syndrome, Velocardiofacial Syndrome (VCFS), or even just 22Q. Despite the different names, it all refers to the same condition.

At its core, 22Q is a genetic condition caused by a tiny missing piece of chromosome 22. It's something a person is born with, and it happens completely by chance in most cases. This tiny missing section can affect different parts of the body, which is why every child with 22Q is different. Some children might have health challenges, while others might have learning differences or speech delays. Some kids have barely any noticeable symptoms at all!

The key thing to remember here is this: no two people with 22Q are the same. Just because you read about one child with certain struggles doesn't mean your child will have them, too. Your child's journey with 22Q is their own, and while there may be bumps along the road, there is also so much hope and support available.

How Does 22Q Happen?

First things first: this is not your fault.

When I first heard that my son had 22Q, I started questioning everything. Did I do something wrong in pregnancy? Could I have prevented this? The answer is no. 22Q happens randomly in about 90% of cases, meaning it just occurred during development. In the other 10% of cases, it is inherited from a parent who also has the deletion, but even then, that parent may have had little to no symptoms themselves.

To understand why 22Q happens, let's do a quick (and simple!) genetics lesson.

Our bodies are made up of trillions of cells, and inside each cell, we have DNA, which is like an instruction manual that tells our bodies how to grow and function. This DNA is packed into 23 pairs of chromosomes—one set from each parent. People with 22Q are missing a tiny piece of chromosome 22 at a location called 22q11.2 (which is just a fancy way of saying "a small part of chromosome 22 is missing"). Because this little section holds important genetic instructions, some body systems—like the heart, immune system, or speech development—might be affected.

That's it! It's simply a missing piece of genetic material, not something anyone caused or could have prevented.

Who Does 22Q Affect?

One of the biggest misconceptions about 22Q is that it's rare. In reality, it affects 1 in every 2,000–4,000 births, making it one of the most common genetic conditions after Down syndrome. It affects all ethnicities and genders equally.

The way 22Q affects someone can range from very mild to more complex. Some children are diagnosed as newborns because they have heart conditions or feeding difficulties (like mine!) Others aren't diagnosed until childhood when they experience speech delays, learning challenges, or immune issues. Some individuals don't even find out until adulthood when they have children of their own and genetic testing is done.

The key takeaway here is: if you've just received this diagnosis, you are not alone. There are thousands of families around the world going through similar experiences, and there is a whole community of support available.

What Medical Terms Should You Know (Without Feeling Overwhelmed)?

When you first read about 22Q, it might feel like there's a huge list of potential issues your child could face—heart defects, immune deficiencies, speech problems, learning differences, and more. It's enough to make any parent feel anxious. But don't let the medical language scare you.

Here's the truth: Your child is your child first. Everything else? That's what the doctors, therapists, and specialists are here for.

Let's break down some of the most common concerns in a simple, non-scary way:

- Heart Defects – Some babies with 22Q are born with heart conditions that may require monitoring or surgery (my own son had open-heart surgery at one year old). The good news? Medical advancements mean these surgeries have high success rates, and many children go on to live full, active lives.
- Speech Delays & Palate Issues – Some kids with 22Q have a cleft palate or struggle with certain speech sounds. Speech therapy and, if needed, palate surgery can make a huge difference.
- Immune System Differences – A weaker immune system might mean more colds or infections, but doctors can help manage this with vaccinations and extra care. For instance, my son was tested for 2 years, and they made sure that if his immune system was strong enough, then he could have his MMR. They also have other options to live vaccinations. I also keep on top of vitmains to give him that extra help! Iron/immune boosts/multi-vitamins/chewy calcium are ones that i use.
- Learning Differences (ADHD, Autism, etc.) – It's true that ADHD and autism traits are more common in kids with 22Q, but that doesn't mean every child will have them. And if they do? There are so many ways to support them, from therapy to medication to simple lifestyle changes.

Just because something is "common" doesn't mean it will definitely be part of you and your child's experience. And if it is, there are ways to help.

What's in a Name? Different Terms for 22Q

Over the years, 22Q has been called many different things, which can be confusing. Here are some of the terms you might come across:

- DiGeorge Syndrome – A name given when immune system issues are present.
- Velocardiofacial Syndrome (VCFS) – Used when speech, heart, and facial differences are involved.
- Shprintzen Syndrome – Named after the doctor who studied speech-related issues in 22Q.
- CATCH22 Syndrome – An old term that is not commonly used anymore.

Today, most doctors just say 22q11.2 deletion syndrome or simply 22Q.

I like to use 22Qutie! Because Jett (my son) is so cute!

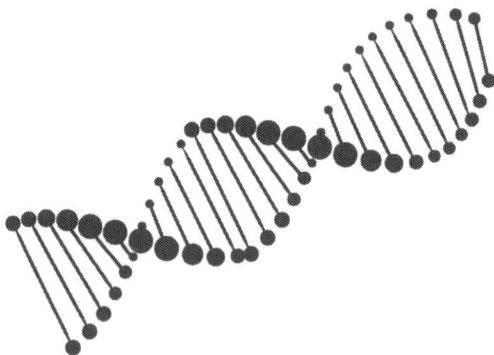

When Jett was diagnosed with 22Q, I was terrified at first. I worried about his future, his health, and what this would mean for our family. But now, years later, I can tell you this: Your child is still the same wonderful, beautiful child they were before you heard the word "22Q." They are not a diagnosis—they are a person full of potential, laughter, and love.

This journey is different from what you may have expected, but it is still filled with joy, progress, and incredible moments you will cherish forever. And through every challenge, you will find strength, support, and so much love.

"You are not alone."

Chapter 2: Diagnosis and First Reactions

The moment I heard the words "Your child has 22q11.2 deletion syndrome," my world completely fell apart.

I remember sitting in that doctor's office, my heart pounding, my hands shaking, struggling to make sense of what I had just been told. It felt like the floor had been ripped out from under me. I couldn't breathe. I couldn't think. I couldn't even cry—because I was too stunned to fully understand what was happening.

In the days and weeks that followed, I went through a rollercoaster of emotions. Shock. Grief. Fear. Numbness. Panic. I was terrified for my son's future, and honestly, for my own. I kept thinking, I can't do this. I'm not strong enough for this.
I couldn't be alone in those first few weeks—I was too scared of my own thoughts. I couldn't look in the cot at night because I was afraid I would find him not breathing. I had PTSD, I needed medication to sleep, and I was prescribed antidepressants just to keep going.

And you know what? That's okay.

If you're feeling anything like I did—overwhelmed, broken, lost, or even physically ill with worry—I need you to hear this: you are not alone, and your feelings are valid.
Let's talk about the diagnosis process, what this means for the future, and most importantly, how you will get through this. Because you will.

How and When Is 22Q Diagnosed?

Some families find out about 22Q before their baby is even born, while others—like me—don't get the diagnosis until after birth, in early childhood, or even later in life. No matter when you receive the news, the emotions are just as powerful.

Prenatal Diagnosis - With advances in genetic testing, some parents find out during pregnancy through Non-Invasive Prenatal Testing (NIPT) or amniocentesis. (At the moment this might be something you need to ask for/pay for). If you received a prenatal diagnosis, you may feel like you're grieving the baby you imagined. But let me tell you this: your baby is still your baby. They are still growing, still moving, still waiting to meet you. And once you hold them, that love will be just as strong—perhaps even stronger—because you will know how much they have already overcome.

Diagnosis in Infancy - Many babies with 22Q are diagnosed shortly after birth, especially if they have:
- A heart defect that requires surgery
- Feeding difficulties (trouble swallowing, weak suck, reflux)
- Low calcium levels causing seizures
- Frequent infections due to immune system differences

This is where many of us get our first taste of medical overwhelm—surgeons, specialists, blood tests, hospital stays. It's terrifying, but the amazing doctors know what they're doing, and your baby will be in good hands.

Diagnosis in Childhood - Some children are diagnosed later, usually when parents notice:
- Speech delays (trouble making certain sounds or a nasal voice)
- Developmental delays (walking or talking later than expected)
- Learning difficulties (struggling with schoolwork or attention)
- Frequent infections (getting sick often and taking longer to recover)

For some families, getting a diagnosis is actually a relief because it explains why their child has been struggling and opens the door to support.

Diagnosis in Adulthood

Some people don't find out they have 22Q until they are adults —sometimes because their child is diagnosed first, leading them to get tested. Adults with 22Q may have mild symptoms they never realized were connected, like anxiety, autoimmune conditions, or a history of learning difficulties.

The Emotional Impact of Diagnosis

Let's be honest: this diagnosis is hard to hear. No parent expects to be told that their child has a genetic condition. It shakes everything you thought you knew about your future.

I remember saying to the doctor, "I can't do this. I am not strong enough for this."

She looked at me kindly and said something that changed everything:

"Your child doesn't need a happy mother right now. He just needs a mother. That's all."

It was like a light switched on. I didn't need to have it all figured out. I didn't need to be positive and strong and full of wisdom. I just needed to be there.

That's what I want to tell you, too. You don't have to be strong right now. You just have to be here.

Coping with the Initial Shock

When the diagnosis first hits, it can feel like you're drowning. Everything suddenly becomes "before the diagnosis" and "after the diagnosis." It's okay to grieve the future you imagined. It's okay to feel broken. But little by little, you will find your way through.

Here's what helped me, and what might help you too:

1. Take It Hour by Hour

At first, even getting through the next five minutes felt impossible. The idea of "taking it one day at a time" was laughable—I couldn't even handle breakfast without crying.

So instead, I took it hour by hour:

- If I got up and made coffee, that was a win.
- If I got dressed, another win.
- If I made it through bedtime, I survived another day.

Each tiny step adds up. One day, you'll realize you're not counting the hours anymore—you're just living again.

2. Find Your Safe People

You don't have to go through this alone. Find one or two people you can call, text, or just sit with when it feels too heavy. Maybe it's your partner, your best friend, or even an online 22Q support group.

3. Ignore Google (For Now)

I know it's tempting, but try not to Google everything at once. You'll read worst-case scenarios that may not even apply to your child. Stick to reliable sources and take things one step at a time.

*I have added some self care sheets at the end of this book to help you through these little wins in the early days of diagnosis.

4. Accept Help

If someone offers to cook a meal, watch your other kids, or just be there—say yes. You don't have to do this alone.

5. Allow Yourself to Feel Everything

There is no wrong way to react to this news. Whether you feel numb, heartbroken, angry, or strangely calm—it's all normal. Cry when you need to. Scream into a pillow if you have to. Let it out.

And if you find yourself struggling to function, talk to a doctor. There is no shame in needing antidepressants, therapy, or extra support. I needed all of those things, and they helped me get through the hardest days.

What This Diagnosis Means for the Future

Right now, it might feel like the future is uncertain, but here's the truth: your child will grow, learn, and surprise you in ways you never imagined.

Yes, there will be challenges. But there will also be joy, laughter, and milestones that feel even more magical because you know how hard they worked for them.

You are stronger than you think. And when you don't feel strong? That's okay. You just need to be there.

Hour by hour, step by step, you will get through this.

Chapter 3: The Spectrum of 22Q Outcomes

One of the most important things I've learned on this journey is that no two children with 22Q are the same (apart from they are all adorable of course).

When you first hear the diagnosis, it's easy to imagine a single path—one set of symptoms, one type of outcome. But 22Q is a spectrum, and just like every child is unique, every 22Q journey is unique too.

Some children have very mild symptoms and may not even realize they have 22Q until later in life. Others have more complex medical needs that require extra support. And then there are children, like my own, who fall somewhere in between.

If you've started Googling (which I completely understand—been there!), you've probably seen a long list of possible symptoms. Some children have many of them, some have just a few. Some need surgeries, others don't. Some struggle with learning or speech delays, while others fly through school.

The thing to remember is this: your child is not a list of symptoms.

Your child is your child.

And whatever challenges they face, there is help, support, and hope.

Mild vs. More Complex Cases

It's natural to wonder: Where does my child fit in? Will they be okay?

Truthfully, it's impossible to know right away. Some babies with complex medical issues in infancy grow into healthy, thriving children. Others who seem to be doing well at first may face challenges as they grow.

Just know that you are strong and you *can* face this journey.

Here's a simple way to think about it:

Mild Cases

- Some people with 22Q don't even know they have it until adulthood.
- They may have minor speech issues, mild learning difficulties, or anxiety.
- No major medical interventions are needed.

More Complex Cases

- Some children need heart surgery, feeding support, or help with speech development.
- They may have immune system issues, low calcium, or developmental delays.
- Some need extra support with learning, behavior, or social skills.

No matter where your child falls on this spectrum, it's okay. Because no matter what challenges you face, there is help and support available.

Common Symptoms & Why They Vary So Much

One of the tricky things about 22Q is that it can look completely different in different people. That's because this tiny missing piece of a chromosome affects many parts of the body—but how it affects each person varies.

Some of the most common symptoms include:

Medical Differences

- Heart conditions (like Tetralogy of Fallot, VSD, or other congenital defects)
- Low calcium levels (causing seizures or muscle twitching in infancy)
- Feeding difficulties (due to low muscle tone or palate differences)
- Frequent infections (due to immune system differences)
- Hearing or vision issues

Development & Learning
- Speech delays or a nasal-sounding voice
- Delayed milestones (walking, talking, coordination)
- Mild to moderate learning difficulties
- ADHD or autism-like traits (but not always!)

Behavior & Emotional Well-Being
- Anxiety (very common in children and adults with 22Q)
- Shyness or social difficulties
- Emotional sensitivity (big feelings that can be overwhelming)

But here's the important part: not every child has every symptom. I know the lists can be scary, but try to remember that your child will be their own person. They may have just a few of these challenges, or they may face more—but either way, you will learn, they will grow, and together you will find your way.

Stories from Other Families
One of the most comforting things I've found on this journey is hearing from other families who have been there.
At first, I wasn't ready. I had to delete Facebook because I wasn't emotionally strong enough to hear other people's stories. It was just too much.
And if that's where you are right now—that is completely okay.
Give yourself time. When you're ready, there are some incredible Facebook groups and online communities filled with parents who understand exactly what you're going through.
Some stories will bring you comfort, some might scare you, and some will fill you with hope. But the one thing they all have in common is this: you are not alone.

Here are just a few stories from families with different 22Q journeys:

Emma's Story – The Surprise Diagnosis

Emma's son, Jake, was diagnosed at three years old after struggling with speech delays and frequent ear infections. She never suspected anything genetic—she just thought he needed extra speech therapy. When they got the diagnosis, she was shocked but relieved to finally have answers. Today, Jake is thriving in school, loves soccer, and has a great group of friends.

♥

Tom's Story – Complex Medical Needs, But a Happy Life

Tom's daughter, Lily, was diagnosed at birth because she had a heart defect that required surgery. The first year was tough, with multiple hospital stays, feeding struggles, and lots of worry. But at five years old, she's a happy, energetic little girl who loves singing and dancing. Tom says, "The journey hasn't been easy, but I wouldn't change her for the world."

♥

Sophie's Story – A Late Diagnosis in Adulthood

Sophie didn't find out she had 22Q until she was 28 years old—after her son was diagnosed. Growing up, she always felt a little different: she had trouble with math, was extremely shy, and had mild scoliosis. But she never knew there was a reason for it. Getting a diagnosis helped her understand herself better, and now she's advocating for awareness in the 22Q community.

Finding Your Own Path

Every child's journey with 22Q is different. Some will need more support, others will need less—but they will all grow into their own unique and wonderful selves.

And no matter what challenges come, there is always:

✓ Medical help available

✓ Therapies to support speech, learning, and behavior

✓ A community of parents who understand

✓ A future filled with love, joy, and milestones that will feel extra special

The best advice I can give you is this:

Take things one step at a time.

Don't compare your child to anyone else.

Celebrate the small victories—they are HUGE.

And when you're ready, know that there is an incredible 22Q community waiting to welcome you. But take your time. This is your journey, and you get to walk it at your own pace.

Part 2: Health, Growth, and Thriving

Chapter 4: Medical Considerations

When you first hear about 22Q, one of the scariest parts can be all the medical possibilities that come with it. The list of potential health concerns can feel overwhelming, but let me reassure you: not every child will have all of these issues. And even if your child does need medical treatment, there are amazing doctors, specialists, and surgeons out there who will guide you every step of the way.

I know this because I've been there.

I remember sitting in a hospital room, staring at my tiny baby, feeling completely helpless. My son was born with a heart defect that required open-heart surgery at one year old. The thought of handing him over to a surgical team felt impossible. How could I trust anyone else to take care of him when he was so fragile?

But here's what I want to share with you—the part I wish someone had told me back then:

 Kids are so much stronger than we realize.
 The recovery will amaze you.
 Scars fade—physically and emotionally.

Two years later, his scar is barely noticeable, and what felt like the hardest thing in the world at the time is now just a small part of his story.

So if you're reading this, worrying about surgeries, hospital stays, or what the future holds—take a deep breath. It's going to be okay. Let's talk about some of the most common medical challenges and how they are managed.

Common Health Concerns in 22Q

Some children with 22Q will have mild medical needs, while others will need extra care. Here are some of the most common health concerns, how they are treated, and what to expect.

1. Heart Defects ♥

How common is it?

Around 75% of children with 22Q have some kind of congenital heart defect. Some are minor and require no treatment, while others need surgery.

Types of heart defects in 22Q:

- Tetralogy of Fallot (TOF) – A condition that affects blood flow through the heart.
- Ventricular Septal Defect (VSD) – A hole between the heart's lower chambers.
- Interrupted Aortic Arch (IAA) – A rare condition where part of the aorta is missing.

My son had open-heart surgery for a VSD and TOF as a baby, and it was the most terrifying experience of my life. The hospital stay lasted two weeks, and the hardest part was the waiting. Seeing him sedated, covered in wires, and connected to machines was heartbreaking.

But the incredible thing? Babies and children recover FAST.

Within days, he was sitting up, smiling, and playing with toys. The scar that I obsessed over at first? Now, two years later, it's barely visible. I spent so much time worrying about it, and yet, it turns out most people don't even notice it unless I point it out! One thing we do in our family is talk openly about scars. We show him our own scars and remind him that everyone has scars—they're just part of our stories.

If your child needs heart surgery, know this: it will be hard, but you will get through it, and your child will amaze you with their strength.

Immune System Differences

Some children with 22Q have weaker immune systems, which means they get sick more often and take longer to recover.

How does it affect daily life?

- More frequent colds, ear infections, and illnesses.
- Some kids need extra vaccinations or immune-boosting treatments.
- In rare cases, children may need special immune support from specialists.

I used to worry constantly about every little cold or cough, but over time I learned that as they grow, their immune system usually strengthens. Always check in with your doctor if your child is getting sick often, but try not to panic.

Cleft Palate & Speech Delays

How common is it?

Around 1 in 3 children with 22Q have some type of palate difference, which can affect speech and feeding. Some children have a visible cleft palate, while others (like my son) have something called velopharyngeal insufficiency (VPI)—where the palate doesn't close properly.

When my son was a baby, I noticed that his tongue would stick out a lot. By 15 months, he still wasn't making clear speech sounds like "D" or "B." That's when we started investigating, and an X-ray confirmed that his palate wasn't closing properly.

As I write this book, we are still waiting for his surgery, but from everything I've heard, the results can be life-changing for speech development. If your child has speech delays, don't lose hope—there are so many ways to help! Hopefully i can update you all soon!

Low Calcium & Seizures

Some babies with 22Q struggle with low calcium levels, which can cause muscle twitching, irritability, and (in rare cases) seizures. What helps?

- Blood tests to check calcium levels.
- Supplements if needed.
- Most kids outgrow this issue over time!

Growth & Feeding Challenges

Many children with 22Q have slow growth or trouble gaining weight. Some may have feeding difficulties, reflux, or food allergies.

Things that help:

- Seeing a nutritionist for advice.
- Thickening feeds for babies with swallowing issues.
- Patience—most kids catch up in their own time!

My son is short for his age, but he's healthy and strong—and that's what matters most. Ask to use a 22Q percentile chart, to get a more accurate idea of how your child is coming along.

The Importance of a Medical Team

One of the best things you can do for your child is to build a strong medical team.

You'll likely have multiple specialists, including:

A pediatrician (to oversee general health)

A cardiologist (for heart care, if needed)

An ENT specialist (for palate or hearing issues)

A speech therapist (to help with communication)

A geneticist (to guide you through 22Q care)

Having a great team makes all the difference. Don't be afraid to ask questions, push for referrals, or seek second opinions. You are your child's best advocate! If you live in the UK like me, the NHS will build an amazing team for you! But knowing this list means that you can make sure you are getting the right care for your child.

Final Thoughts: One Step at a Time

If you've made it this far, trust me i know this all sounds like a lot.
But here's what I've learned: you don't have to deal with everything at once.
Take it step by step.
Trust that your child will show you what they need.
Remember that medicine has come so far, and there is help for every challenge.
Most of all, never forget that your child is still just your child —not a diagnosis, not a medical case, but a beautiful, strong, and resilient little person.
And they will surprise you every single day.

Speech and Feeding Challenges
One of the things I didn't expect when my son was diagnosed with 22Q was how much it would affect speech and feeding. At first, I thought he was just taking his time—some kids are late talkers, right? But as the months went by, I noticed things that made me wonder if something else was going on.
His tongue would stick out a lot as a baby. He didn't babble as much as other babies his age. And by 15 months, he wasn't making clear sounds like "D" or "B." That's when we started looking into speech development and learned that 22Q can cause delays in both feeding and talking.
If you're facing this with your own child, I want you to know: you are not alone. Speech delays are very common in children with 22Q, and there is so much help available. It can take time, patience, and sometimes even surgery, but your child will find their voice—in their own way and at their own pace.
Let's break it down and talk about what to expect and how to help.

Speech Delays in 22Q

About 70-90% of children with 22Q will have some kind of speech delay. This can range from mild pronunciation difficulties to severe speech impairment. The good news? There are therapies, surgeries, and interventions that can make a huge difference.

Why do children with 22Q struggle with speech?

There are a few different reasons:

Palate Differences – Many kids with 22Q have a cleft palate or a condition called velopharyngeal insufficiency (VPI), which means the soft palate doesn't close properly when speaking. This can cause nasal-sounding speech or difficulty forming certain sounds.

Low Muscle Tone – Some kids with 22Q have weaker muscles in the mouth, jaw, and tongue, making it harder to form words clearly.

Hearing Issues – Frequent ear infections and fluid buildup can make it harder for children to hear speech properly, which can delay their ability to imitate sounds.

Brain Processing Differences – Some children with 22Q have mild learning delays or ADHD/autism traits, which can make language development slower.

Signs of Speech Delay in 22Q

- Not babbling much as a baby
- Difficulty making certain sounds (like "D," "B," "P")
- Speech sounds nasal or unclear
- Struggles to put words together into sentences
- Gets frustrated trying to communicate

Every child is different—some start talking later, while others need therapy or surgery to help with speech.

Speech Therapy: What Help Is Available?

If your child has speech delays, early intervention is key. The sooner therapy starts, the more progress they can make!

Types of Speech Therapy

Traditional Speech Therapy – A speech therapist helps your child practice sounds and build language skills through play and structured exercises.

Oral Motor Therapy – Exercises to strengthen the tongue, lips, and jaw muscles to improve speech clarity.

Resonance Therapy – If your child has nasal-sounding speech, special therapy techniques can help improve airflow and articulation.

Sign Language or Picture Boards – Some children benefit from alternative communication methods while they're developing speech skills.

Tip: If you're waiting for speech therapy appointments, try narrating your day to your child: "We're putting on shoes now! Look, here's your cup!" The more they hear language, the better!

Surgery for Speech: When Is It Needed?

If your child has a cleft palate or VPI, speech therapy alone may not be enough. Surgery can help improve speech clarity by correcting the structure of the palate.

We noticed early on that our son wasn't making certain sounds and his tongue stuck out a lot. An X-ray showed that his palate wasn't closing properly, which meant that air was escaping through his nose when he tried to speak.

As I write this book, we are still waiting for his palate surgery, and I won't lie—it's a little nerve-wracking. But I've spoken to many parents whose children had this surgery, and they say the improvement in speech is incredible.

If your child is recommended for palate surgery, it's okay to feel nervous. But just like with heart surgery, children recover so quickly, and the results can be life-changing.

Feeding Difficulties in 22Q

Speech delays and feeding issues often go hand in hand. Some babies with 22Q struggle to breastfeed or bottle-feed, while others have trouble with chewing and swallowing as they grow.

Common Feeding Challenges

Weak suck or trouble latching (due to low muscle tone or cleft palate)

Gagging or choking on certain textures

Milk or food coming out of the nose (if the palate doesn't close properly)

Difficulty chewing solid foods

It can be really frustrating watching your child struggle with feeding, but there are lots of ways to help.

Tips for Feeding a Child with 22Q

Try different bottle types – Some babies need special bottles that help with suction, like the Dr. Brown's Specialty Bottle or the Haberman Feeder.

Introduce new textures slowly – Some kids need time to adjust to different textures—don't rush it!

Use thickened liquids – If your child has trouble swallowing thin liquids, doctors may recommend thickening formula, milk, or water to make it easier to swallow.

Oral Motor Therapy – Exercises can help strengthen the tongue and jaw muscles for better chewing and swallowing.

Let your child explore food – If they seem hesitant, let them play with food first. Sometimes touching and smelling new foods helps them feel more comfortable.

Tip: If mealtimes feel stressful, take a break and don't force it. Some kids need extra time, and that's okay. As long as they're growing and getting the nutrition they need, they'll get there in their own time.

Final Thoughts: Progress Happens!

I know how overwhelming it can feel when your child isn't talking yet or struggles to eat. It's easy to compare them to other kids and wonder when things will "catch up."

But here's the truth: every child moves at their own pace.

Some kids with 22Q talk late, but then catch up beautifully.

Some need speech therapy or surgery, but then make amazing progress.

Some have feeding struggles early on but grow into happy, healthy eaters.

I've learned that every small step forward is a huge victory. The first time my son said "Mama," I cried. The first time he ate a new food without gagging, I cheered. These moments might seem small to others, but to us, they are everything.

So if you're feeling worried right now, hold onto hope. Your child's voice will come. Their confidence will grow. And no matter how long it takes, they will get there—with you cheering them on every step of the way.

Chapter 6: Learning and Development

If there's one thing I've learned as a parent of a child with 22Q, it's this: our kids are full of surprises.

One day, they might struggle with something you thought would come naturally—like learning to say their first words. The next day, they do something incredible—like sensing when you're sad and bringing you a tissue, giving the biggest, warmest hug, or making you laugh just when you need it most. Parenting a child with 22Q is a rollercoaster of "Wow, I didn't expect that!" moments. And when it comes to learning and development, the journey can be just as unpredictable.

Common Learning Challenges in 22Q

Okay, let's get the big scary words out of the way:

ADHD

Autism traits

Speech and language delays

Processing difficulties

Memory struggles

I remember when these words were first given to me. It felt like someone had handed me a medical dictionary and told me to memorize it overnight. I panicked. I googled. (Pro tip: never google when you're already stressed!)

But here's the thing i found: most people are "a little bit" something.

Seriously, go into any office or school and you'll find adults who forget their keys daily (ADHD), people who prefer talking to their cat over humans (autism traits), and those who can't follow a set of directions to save their lives (processing issues).

Our kids might have some learning challenges, yes. But that doesn't define who they are—it just means we might need to tweak the way we teach them. And the good news? There are tons of ways to help them thrive.

How Children with 22Q Learn Best

Every child learns in their own way, at their own pace, and children with 22Q are no different. Some things may take longer, and some skills might require extra support, but they can and will learn. It's about meeting them where they are, celebrating their progress, and providing the tools they need to succeed.

■ Visual Learning Can Be a Powerful Tool
Many children with 22Q find it easier to process information
when they can see it rather than just hear it. Visual aids like
pictures, charts, or demonstrations can help them understand
and remember what they need to do.

For example, if getting dressed is a challenge, a simple picture
checklist can be a great support:

Underwear
Socks
Pants
Shirt

Visual cues can take away frustration and make everyday tasks
feel more manageable.

Repetition Helps Information Stick
Many children with 22Q have difficulties with working
memory, which means they may need more time and practice
to retain information.

If something doesn't seem to "stick" right away, that's okay.
Repeating things in a gentle, encouraging way helps build
understanding over time.

For example, if you're teaching a new word, you might need to
repeat it several times before it becomes familiar. And even if
it takes longer than expected, they will get there. The key is
patience, consistency, and reassurance.

Routine Brings Comfort and Confidence

Children with 22Q often thrive on structure. Knowing what to expect helps them feel safe and in control. Having a consistent daily routine can make a big difference.

Some ways to create structure include:

- Using a visual schedule with pictures of daily activities
- Giving a gentle warning before transitions (e.g., "In five minutes, we'll get ready for bed")
- Keeping meal times, bedtime, and activities as predictable as possible

Of course, life isn't always predictable, and some days won't go as planned. That's okay. Flexibility is important too—it's about finding a balance that works for both you and your child.

Encouraging Strengths & Supporting Challenges

When my son was first diagnosed, I worried so much about what he might struggle with that I didn't immediately see all the things he was already so wonderful at. For every challenge, there is also a strength. Our children might face obstacles, but they also have qualities that make them truly special.

Common Strengths in Children with 22Q

Deep empathy – Many children with 22Q are incredibly sensitive and caring. They notice when someone is sad and offer comfort, whether it's a hug, a gentle touch, or simply being present.

Strong determination – They work incredibly hard to achieve their goals, even if it takes a little longer. Their perseverance is inspiring.

Unique creativity – Whether it's through art, music, or imaginative play, children with 22Q often have their own special way of expressing themselves.

Resilience – They go through challenges—sometimes medical, sometimes developmental—but their ability to keep going is something to be admired.

How to Support Challenges
Every child has areas where they need extra support. The good news is that there are many strategies and resources available to help.

If attention is a challenge (like ADHD)...
- Keep instructions short and simple.
- Break tasks into small, manageable steps.
- Allow for movement breaks to help with focus.

If social skills are difficult...
- Practice role-playing common social situations (e.g., saying hello to a friend).
- Use social stories (short, simple picture books showing different interactions).
- Celebrate small wins, like making eye contact or taking turns in a game.

If reading and writing are hard...
- Try audiobooks or let them trace letters in sand, shaving cream, or rice for sensory learning.
- Use speech-to-text tools if writing is frustrating.
- Choose short books with engaging pictures to make reading fun.

If memory is tricky...
- Use songs, rhymes, or repetition to reinforce learning.
- Provide visual reminders (like sticky notes, charts, or labeled objects).
- Be patient—sometimes information just needs more time to settle in.

Final Thoughts: Celebrate Every Win

Parenting a child with 22Q is a journey with its ups and downs. Some days, it may feel overwhelming. But every step forward is a victory, no matter how small.

The first time they communicate what they want—even nonverbally? That's a huge moment.

The day they master a new skill, no matter how long it took? That's incredible.

The little moments of joy, laughter, and connection? Those are what truly matter.

The path may not be what you expected, but it is still beautiful. Take it one step at a time, and know that you are not alone. Your child is growing, learning, and finding their own way in the world—with you right beside them.

Mental Health and Emotional Well-being

When my son was diagnosed with 22Q, I was so focused on the physical challenges—the heart surgery, the feeding difficulties, the upcoming palate repair—that I didn't even stop to think about the emotional impact. Not just on him, but on me, too.

It wasn't until months later, when the shock started to wear off, that I realized how deeply the diagnosis had affected my mental health. I was constantly anxious. I couldn't sleep. I was terrified something would happen to him. I would wake up in the night and check that he was breathing. I couldn't be alone for even a moment because the silence made me panic.

That was the moment I started to shift my mindset. I had spent so much time trying to fight my emotions, trying to push them away, trying to be "strong" when really, I just needed to allow myself to feel everything—the grief, the fear, the exhaustion—without judgment.

This is where ACT therapy (Acceptance and Commitment Therapy) changed everything for me.

Using ACT Therapy to Support Myself (and My Child)

ACT therapy is all about accepting your emotions rather than fighting them. Instead of trying to force myself to "think positive" when I felt terrified, I learned to say, "This is hard, and that's okay."

Instead of telling myself, "I shouldn't feel like this," I started saying, "Of course I feel like this. This is a huge change. But I can still show up for my child."

Navigating Mental Health Challenges in Children with 22Q

As my son grew, I realized that he, too, would need emotional support. 22Q doesn't just affect physical health—it can also impact mental health.

Many children with 22Q experience:

Anxiety – Fear of new situations, separation anxiety, or trouble handling change.

Frustration – Difficulty communicating can lead to meltdowns or emotional outbursts.

Social struggles – Some children find it hard to connect with peers, especially if they have autism traits.

Attention and focus challenges – Many children have ADHD or trouble processing information quickly.

For my son, the hardest part has been communication. He doesn't speak yet, and that has been one of my greatest struggles as a parent.

There have been times when he has been screaming, crying, completely distressed—and I haven't been able to figure out why. Does he need something? Is he in pain? Is he just frustrated? It is heartbreaking to not be able to help your own child because you don't know what they need.

I won't lie—this part has been really hard. There have been moments when I've sat on the floor, crying with him, feeling utterly helpless.

But here's what I want you to know: it does get better. I had to learn new ways to connect with my son—through gestures, pictures, and even just reading his eyes and expressions. We started using PECS (Picture Exchange Communication System), and I can't tell you how amazing it felt the first time he handed me a picture of a drink because he was thirsty. It was a small moment, but it was everything.

If you are struggling with a non-verbal child, please know that they will find their way to communicate. And so will you.

How to Support Your Child's Emotional Well-being
Give Them a Voice (Even If They Don't Speak Yet)
- Use pictures, sign language, or communication devices to help them express themselves.
- Even if they don't speak, talk to them constantly—they understand more than you think.
- Watch for their body language and cues—they are always communicating, just in their own way.

Create a Safe, Predictable Environment
Children with 22Q thrive on routine. It helps them feel secure and in control.
- Use visual schedules to help them understand what's coming next.
- Give gentle warnings before transitions (e.g., "In five minutes, we're leaving for school").
- Create calming spaces with weighted blankets or sensory tools if they get overwhelmed.

Help Them Manage Anxiety
Many kids with 22Q experience anxiety. Here are some things that have helped us:
- Deep breathing exercises – Practice slow, deep breaths together.
- Comfort objects – A favorite stuffed toy, blanket, or fidget can help.
- Sensory breaks – Sometimes, just stepping away from a situation can make a difference.

Build Their Confidence
For every challenge, children with 22Q have incredible strengths too.
Many have an amazing memory.
 They are deeply caring and empathetic.
They have a strong determination—you will be amazed at how hard they work! Focus on what they can do, and remind them (and yourself) that progress, no matter how small, is still progress.

Taking Care of Your Own Mental Health

You can't pour from an empty cup. If you're feeling overwhelmed, you are not alone.

Find a support network – Whether it's a therapist, a friend, or an online group, talking to others who understand can be a lifeline.

Give yourself permission to feel – It's okay to be sad, scared, or frustrated. Let yourself feel it, then keep going.

Take small breaks – Even five minutes of deep breathing, a warm cup of tea, or stepping outside can help.

Know when to ask for help – If you feel overwhelmed, please reach out to a doctor or therapist.

Remember to have fun - go out with friends, plan trips if you can. Give yourself things to look forward to.

Final Thoughts: You Are Enough

Some days, this journey will feel impossibly hard. But you are stronger than you think.

I want you to know that no matter how difficult the early days feel, you will find your way. You will learn to understand your child in ways that no one else can. And they will teach you things about love, patience, and resilience that you never imagined.

So when you feel overwhelmed, remember: You don't have to be perfect. You just have to be there. And that is enough.

Part 3: Family, School & Social Life

Parenting a Child with 22Q

Parenting a child with 22Q is a journey filled with love, learning, and a whole lot of patience. Some days are beautiful, some days are overwhelming, and some days are a mix of both. But through it all, I've learned that even the smallest victories matter.

Daily Life and Routines - Routine is everything in our house. It helps my son feel safe, and honestly, it helps me feel more in control too.

Morning Routine – Mornings can be tough with three boys, so we keep things predictable. A visual schedule helps my 22Qutie know what's coming next. I also give extra time for transitions because rushing only leads to frustration.

Mealtime – Feeding issues are common with 22Q, and my son definitely has his struggles. Most days all he will eat are peanut butter sandwiches, other times banana is the only thing he'll accept. And that's okay. We celebrate small wins, like trying a new texture or using a fork.

Bedtime – This is my favorite part of the day. Sometimes a warm bath, a bedtime story (even if I'm the only one doing the talking), and lots of cuddles. No matter how tough the day has been, we always end it with love.

Encouraging Independence - I used to do everything for my son because I didn't want him to struggle. But I've learned that even though things take him longer, he CAN do them—and the sense of pride he gets from doing something himself is priceless.

Getting dressed? He might put his shirt on backward, but he did it himself. Victory.

Peeling a banana? Took him five minutes, but he got there. Victory.

Handing the money to the cashier? A small step toward independence. Victory. It's not about perfection; it's about progress.

Celebrating Milestones
Every parent celebrates their child's first steps, first words, first "I love you." But with a 22Q child, these moments are even more profound.
My son still can't talk, but I will never forget the first time he signed "more" when he wanted another snack. I cried. It was like hearing "Mama" for the first time.
These moments may take longer, but when they come, they are MAGICAL.

Sibling and Family Dynamics
When my son was diagnosed, I worried not just about him but about his siblings too. How would they react? Would they feel left out? Would they understand?

Helping Siblings Understand 22Q
Kids are incredibly resilient, but they also need honesty.
Explaining in simple terms – "Your brother has something called 22Q, which means he needs extra help with some things, but he's still the same amazing little guy."
Encouraging empathy – We talk about how everyone has strengths and challenges. My other children now proudly explain to people, "He's perfect, he just has some extra bits."
Strengthening Family Bonds
There were times I worried my other kids weren't getting enough attention because I was so focused on hospital appointments, therapy sessions, and daily challenges. But I learned that quality time matters more than quantity.
One-on-one time – Even 10 minutes of playing, reading, or chatting makes a difference. Involving siblings – Letting them be part of therapy sessions or doctor's appointments makes them feel included rather than left out.
Celebrating everyone's milestones – Not just our 22Q child's, but their siblings' achievements too.

Navigating School and Education

School is a big decision, and let me tell you—I am TERRIFIED about sending my son. Will they understand him? Will he be supported? Will he be happy?

<u>Choosing the Right School</u>

Every child with 22Q is different. Some thrive in mainstream schools, while others do better in specialized settings.

<u>Mainstream School</u> – If your child can manage with extra support, this can be a great option. Look for schools with strong SEN (Special Educational Needs) teams.

<u>Special Education School</u> – Smaller class sizes, specialized teachers, and a more tailored approach can make a huge difference for some kids.

There's no right or wrong choice—just what's best for your child.

Getting an IEP or EHCP

If your child has 22Q, they are entitled to extra support. In the UK, this comes in the form of an EHCP (Educational Health Care Plan), while in other places, it's called an IEP (Individualized Education Plan).

Advocating for Your Child – Schools don't always offer support unless you push for it. Don't be afraid to fight for what your child needs. You are their voice.

Working with Teachers

Educate them about 22Q—most teachers haven't heard of it!

Keep communication open—regular updates help both sides.

Be realistic—there will be good days and bad days, but having a supportive teacher makes all the difference.

Friendships and Social Skills

One of my biggest fears was: Will my son make friends? Now he is at nursery, i worry a little less as he has some friends already!

Children with 22Q can sometimes struggle with social skills, but that doesn't mean they don't want to connect. They just need a little extra help.

<u>Helping Your Children Develop Social Confidence</u>

Playdates with patient, kind children – Not every child will "get" your child, and that's okay. Find the ones who do.

Using social stories – Simple picture books that teach social skills in a way that makes sense.

Practicing simple interactions – Saying "hi," taking turns, and making eye contact can be learned over time.

Addressing Bullying and Inclusion

Let's be real—some kids can be unkind. I dread the day my son gets teased for being different. But here's what I focus on:

Building his confidence so he knows he is amazing just as he is.

Teaching him to self-advocate (even in non-verbal ways).

Educating his teachers and classmates about 22Q so they can be allies instead of bystanders.

Building a Support Network

Find local parent groups—they are a lifeline.

Join 22Q Facebook communities (when you're ready).

Connect with other families—knowing you're not alone makes all the difference.

Final Thoughts

This journey is not easy.

But it is full of love, growth, and resilience. Somedays, you will feel exhausted, frustrated, and even heartbroken. But other days, you will see your child do something you never thought possible, and it will take your breath away.

So take it one step at a time. Celebrate the small wins. And remember: you are doing an incredible job.

Adolescence and Adulthood

As a parent of a three-year-old with 22q11.2 Deletion Syndrome, I haven't yet walked the path of adolescence and adulthood with my son. But like many of you, I've found myself wondering what the future holds. What will puberty be like for him? How independent will he be? What kind of job could he have? Will he find love and friendship?

The unknowns can be overwhelming, but through research, speaking with specialists, and hearing from other parents further along this journey, I've come to understand that—just like childhood—adolescence and adulthood with 22Q are full of challenges, yes, but also full of possibilities, growth, and unexpected joys. Every child's journey is unique, and while we can't predict exactly what lies ahead, we can prepare, advocate, and support our children as they take each step toward adulthood.

<u>Transitioning to Adolescence</u>
Puberty and Hormonal Changes

One of the things I've learned from other parents is that puberty for children with 22Q can sometimes be delayed or follow a slightly different course. Doctors have told me that hormone imbalances, such as thyroid issues, can be more common in kids with 22Q, so regular check-ups will be important.

Some parents have shared that puberty brings new emotional challenges—mood swings, frustration, and anxiety can sometimes increase. But others say that, while certain aspects are tricky, their kids have handled the transition just fine with support and guidance. Just like everything else with 22Q, each child is different.

<u>What's helped other families?</u>

Talking about changes early and often. Using simple, clear explanations about bodily changes can help prepare them.
Visuals and social stories. Books and visual guides can make the information more accessible.
A supportive medical team. Endocrinologists and pediatricians can monitor hormone levels and overall development.

<u>Supporting Independence and Decision-Making</u>
Something I've learned already as a parent is how important it is to let our children try things for themselves, even if it takes longer or they need extra help. Other parents have reassured me that fostering independence in small ways from a young age—choosing between two snack options, putting on their own shoes, or tidying up toys—can lay the groundwork for bigger decisions later on.
As children grow, helping them with:
✓ Basic self-care skills (dressing, hygiene, meal prep)
✓ Understanding money and budgeting
✓ Learning how to communicate their needs
✓ Practicing problem-solving and decision-making
can help prepare them for more independence in adulthood.

<u>Planning for Adulthood</u>
Even though my son is still small, I know that one day we will need to think about his future—his career, where he will live, and how we can best support him in adulthood. You can start to think about this long before they reach 18 if it makes you feel better to plan!

Career Options and Workplace Support

Many adults with 22Q lead fulfilling working lives. Some parents have shared that their children thrive in structured, routine-based environments, while others do well in creative fields. Some possible career paths that suit different strengths include:

- Office or administrative roles (data entry, reception work)
- Retail or hospitality jobs (working with customers, sorting stock)
- Creative fields (art, music, design, photography)
- Tech-related jobs (coding, IT support, digital content creation)

In the UK, organizations like Mencap offer employment support, and in the USA, The Arc provides career resources for individuals with disabilities.

Workplace accommodations, such as clear instructions, supportive supervisors, and flexible working conditions, can make a huge difference in helping adults with 22Q succeed.

Independent Living vs. Assisted Living

This is a big question for many parents: Will my child be able to live independently? And the truth is, it varies widely. Some adults with 22Q live completely independently with a job, a home, and even a family of their own. Others may need assisted living arrangements or continued parental support.

Some parents have shared that their children thrive in supported living programs, where they have some independence but also access to help when needed.

Planning early—teaching daily life skills, setting up a financial plan, and exploring housing options—can help create a smoother transition when the time comes.

Legal Considerations (Guardianship, Disability Benefits)
Understanding what financial and legal support is available is so important. Here's what I've learned about benefits:

- In the UK:
  - Personal Independence Payment (PIP) can help with living costs. More information is available at gov.uk.
  - Employment and Support Allowance (ESA) helps those who cannot work full-time due to a condition.
  - Access to Work provides support for employment-related needs.
  - Social Security Scotland - Child Disability Payment
  - Social Security Scotland - Carers allowance
  - Carers allowance for England & Wales is part of Universal Credit.
  - High rate disability means that you may be entitled to a blue badge for your car, and a Motobility car.
- In the USA:
  - Supplemental Security Income (SSI) provides financial aid. Learn more at the Social Security Administration.
  - Vocational Rehabilitation Services help individuals with disabilities find employment.

*The above information is just what i have researched, you may know more or find other means of support and thats great! This is just to give you a little starting point.

Relationships and Dating
As parents, we want our children to have fulfilling social lives, to make friends, and to experience love and connection if they want to. Many parents I've spoken to say that, while friendships and romantic relationships can sometimes be more complicated for individuals with 22Q, they are absolutely possible.

Social and Romantic Relationships

Children with 22Q often have strong emotions and deep empathy, but social interactions may be tricky. I have found that my non-verbal son is very social, and this is from developing his social skills early—through nursery, playdates, and structured activities— hopefully this helps towards making friendships easier later on.

For those older teens or adults who do explore romantic relationships, open conversations about trust, boundaries, and communication are essential. Some adults with 22Q marry and have families, while others are happy with close friendships and companionships.

<u>Navigating Love and Trust</u>

From my research, it seems dating with 22Q requires the same things as for anyone else—self-confidence, social opportunities, and support. Some people may need extra guidance in understanding emotions and relationships, but love and companionship are absolutely within reach.

Final Thoughts

Even though my son is still little, I know that one day he will be a teenager, and then an adult. I don't know yet exactly what his future will look like, but I do know this: He will learn and grow in his own time. He will face challenges, but he will also have strengths that make him special. He will find his place in the world, with the right support and love.

If you are like me—still at the beginning of this journey— know that you are not alone. There are parents ahead of us who have walked this path and can offer wisdom and reassurance. There are specialists and support groups to guide us. And most of all, there are our children—full of potential, full of joy, and ready to show us just how incredible they can be.

We are in this together.

Part 4: Support Networks and Charities

One of the biggest lessons I've learned on this journey is that you don't have to do it alone. There is a whole community out there—other parents, support groups, charities, and professionals—who truly understand and are ready to help. When my son was first diagnosed, I felt completely lost. I didn't know where to turn or who to ask for help. But over time, I started to find resources that not only provided information but also gave me a sense of hope. Charities and support networks have been a lifeline for so many families, offering everything from practical advice and financial assistance to emotional support and lifelong connections.

I want you to know that whatever challenge you're facing— whether it's understanding your child's medical needs, accessing education support, or just needing someone to listen —there are organizations out there that care and want to help.

The Importance of Early Intervention

Before we dive into the charities and support networks, I cannot stress this enough: If you have any concerns about your child's development, whether it's speech, feeding, mobility, or learning, talk to your healthcare team as early as possible.

Early intervention makes a huge difference. The sooner your child gets the right therapies and support, the better their chances of reaching their full potential. Whether it's speech therapy, occupational therapy, or educational support, getting started early can make life easier for both your child and your family.

So if you ever have that little voice in your head saying, something doesn't seem right, trust your instincts. Ask questions. Push for assessments. Seek out support. You are your child's best advocate.

Charities and Support Networks in the UK
Max Appeal – www.maxappeal.org.uk
What they do:
- A UK-based charity specifically for families affected by 22Q.
- Offers parent support groups, resources, and guidance on medical and educational needs.
- Provides advocacy and helps families access the right services.
- Organizes family events and meet-ups to connect people within the 22Q community.

Why they're helpful:

Max Appeal helped me realize I wasn't alone. Even just reading other families' stories on their website gave me reassurance. It's a great place to start if you're looking for a sense of community and expert advice.

Unique (Rare Chromosome Disorder Support Group)
www.rarechromo.org
What they do:
- Provides detailed information guides on rare chromosome disorders, including 22Q.
- Offers support to families and individuals affected by genetic conditions.
- Helps with navigating health care, education, and social support services.

Why they're helpful:
They have fantastic in-depth guides about 22Q that explain everything in simple terms. If you ever feel overwhelmed by medical jargon, this is a great resource to help break things down.

Contact (For Families with Disabled Children)
www.contact.org.uk
What they do:
- Provides financial advice, including help with Disability Living Allowance (DLA) and Carer's Allowance.
- Helps parents understand their rights and navigate the healthcare and education system.
- Runs parent support groups where you can connect with other families.

Why they're helpful:
If you're trying to figure out which benefits you're entitled to or need help filling out forms, Contact is an amazing resource. They also have a helpline where you can speak to someone directly.

Mencap – www.mencap.org.uk
What they do:
- Supports individuals with learning disabilities, including those with 22Q.
- Provides employment support, helping people with disabilities find jobs.
- Offers legal advice on things like guardianship and benefits.

Why they're helpful:

If you're thinking about the long-term future and how to support your child into adulthood, Mencap has a lot of valuable resources on work, housing, and independent living.

Contact (For Families with Disabled Children)
www.contact.org.uk
What they do:

- Provides financial advice, including help with Disability Living Allowance (DLA) and Carer's Allowance.
- Helps parents understand their rights and navigate the healthcare and education system.
- Runs parent support groups where you can connect with other families.

Why they're helpful:
If you're trying to figure out which benefits you're entitled to or need help filling out forms, Contact is an amazing resource. They also have a helpline where you can speak to someone directly.

Mencap – www.mencap.org.uk
What they do:

- Supports individuals with learning disabilities, including those with 22Q.
- Provides employment support, helping people with disabilities find jobs.
- Offers legal advice on things like guardianship and benefits.

Why they're helpful:

If you're thinking about the long-term future and how to support your child into adulthood, Mencap has a lot of valuable resources on work, housing, and independent living.

Charities and Support Networks in the USA
The 22Q Family Foundation – www.22qfamilyfoundation.org
What they do:

- Offers free educational resources for parents, educators, and medical professionals.
- Provides scholarships for individuals with 22Q.
- Runs Facebook support groups for parents and individuals living with 22Q.

Why they're helpful:
Their online support groups are a great place to connect with families who truly understand what you're going through.

The International 22Q11.2 Foundation – www.22q.org
What they do:
- Provides detailed medical information about 22Q.
- Connects families with specialists and research studies.
- Hosts annual conferences where families can meet experts and each other.

Why they're helpful:
They're a fantastic source of up-to-date medical research and expert advice. If you're ever looking for the latest information about 22Q, this is the place to go.

The Arc – www.thearc.org
What they do:

- Advocates for disability rights, including education, employment, and housing support.
- Provides legal resources for parents navigating guardianship and disability benefits.
- Supports inclusion and accessibility for individuals with disabilities.

Why they're helpful:
If you ever feel like you need to fight for your child's rights in school or in the workplace, The Arc is a great organization for advocacy and legal support.

Final Thoughts: You Are Not Alone
I know firsthand how overwhelming it can be to navigate all the medical, educational, and emotional challenges that come with 22Q. But please remember: help is out there.
There are parents who have walked this journey before you and are ready to support you.
There are charities and organizations dedicated to making life easier for you and your child.
There are specialists who care deeply and want to help your child thrive.
If you take just one thing away from this chapter, let it be this: reach out, ask for help, and know that you are not alone. There is a whole community ready to lift you up. And together, we can help our incredible children live full, happy, and meaningful lives.

So, You Made It to the End of the Book!

First of all—take a deep breath.

Let that sink in. You've just walked through an entire book about 22Q, from those first terrifying moments of diagnosis to imagining the future for your child. That is no small thing. If no one has told you this yet today: you are doing an amazing job.

This journey—our journey—is not the one we expected, but that doesn't mean it won't be beautiful. It might not look like what we imagined when we first held our little ones in our arms, but what if it turns out to be something even more special? What if this path, though different, brings more love, more growth, and more joy than we ever thought possible?

I started this book because I was once where you are. I know the fear, the confusion, the grief for the life you thought your child would have. I also know the love, the joy, and the pride that come with raising a child with 22Q. I know that the worry never fully goes away, but I also know that hope, strength, and happiness grow alongside it. Let's take a moment to reflect on everything we've covered—from that first diagnosis to the future.

If you're reading this, chances are you've already lived through the hardest part—hearing those words for the first time. Maybe it was in a hospital room, maybe it was over the phone, or maybe it was after months (or even years) of searching for answers. However it happened, I want you to know:

You are not alone. Thousands of families have stood exactly where you are, feeling the same overwhelming emotions.

Every feeling you had (or are still having) is valid. Maybe you cried, maybe you went numb, maybe you felt guilty for grieving while also loving your child so much it hurt. I felt all of those things too.

Your child is still your child. That diagnosis doesn't change who they are—it just gives you the knowledge and tools to support them in the best way possible.

The hardest part about parenting a child with 22Q is the unknowns—how will they develop? What medical issues will they face? Will they talk, walk, make friends? These questions can feel like an enormous weight on your chest.

But here's what I've learned from my own experience and from meeting so many other incredible 22Q families:

Children with 22Q are resilient, determined, and full of joy.

They do things in their own time. Some talk early, some talk later. Some walk early, some need extra support. And all of it is okay.

There is no "right" path. Every child with 22Q is different. Some will need heart surgery, some won't. Some will have speech delays, some won't. Comparing your child to others will only steal the joy of watching them grow into exactly who they are meant to be.

For me, one of the biggest struggles has been navigating life with a child who cannot speak yet. The world can be so verbal, and it's hard not knowing exactly what my child is thinking or feeling. It's easy to feel lost in those moments. But I have learned that communication is so much bigger than words. My child can show love in a hug, bring me tissues when I'm sad, make me laugh with a silly face, and teach me more about patience, understanding, and connection than I ever thought possible.

If your child is nonverbal or has speech delays, I want you to know: they are still telling you who they are every single day. Keep listening, even when the words aren't there yet.

Looking After Yourself as a Parent

One of the biggest lessons I've learned is that you cannot pour from an empty cup. Your child needs you to be strong, but also kind to yourself. You are not just a caregiver—you are a person with your own needs, dreams, and emotions.
One thing that truly helped me was ACT Therapy (Acceptance and Commitment Therapy). It taught me:

To accept my emotions instead of fighting them—fear, sadness, and grief are part of this journey, and it's okay to feel them.

To focus on what I can control—I can't control my child's medical challenges, but I can control how I show up for them each day.

To live in the moment—instead of worrying about the future, I try to celebrate every small victory right now.

If you are struggling with your mental health, please reach out —to a therapist, a support group, or even just a trusted friend. You are not alone, and you deserve support too.

I have also added some self care pages at the back of this book, for you to use in those early moments. Mark those wins! You got out of bed? Thats a win! You smiled today? Thats a win! Celebrate each hour if you have to. You will get there.

Final Thoughts: We Are in This Together

So, here we are at the end of this book. If I could leave you with just one thing, it would be this:

You are not alone.

Your child is not their diagnosis—they are a unique, incredible person with so much to give to this world.

This journey might not be what we expected, but that doesn't mean it won't be full of love, growth, and happiness.

Thank you for being here.
Thank you for walking this path alongside me. Let's all be there for each other—because together, we are stronger. If you need any help or support please email me at:

kates22crew@gmail.com

I will try and help or guide you in any way i can!

The following pages have self care guides, and also medical note entries, so that you can keep information about 22Q specialist appointments, doctors names and numbers in one place. I hope it helps you!

Katy x

Useful Journal Pages:

Please use the following pages to write important medical notes or medical team names and numbers, and to make sure that you remember to check off self care! You matter!

TAKE IT TASK BY TASK AND HOUR BY HOUR. THESE ARE ALL BIG WINS WHEN YOU ARE STRUGGLING! CELEBRATE EVERY TICK!

Self CARE

- ◯ Take a deep breath
- ◯ Have a cup of tea/coffee/hot chocolate
- ◯ Smile!
- ◯ Get out of bed
- ◯ Get Dressed
- ◯ Cuddle your child
- ◯ Phone someone who comforts you
- ◯ Go for a walk
- ◯ Listen to uplifting music
- ◯ Talk about your feelings
- ◯ Plan a coffee or night out or even trip away!
- ◯ Prioritise a self care skin routine
- ◯ Have the cake

TAKE IT TASK BY TASK AND HOUR BY HOUR. USE THESE BLANK PAGES TO MAKE YOUR OWN WINS!

Self CARE

- ○ ....
- ○ ....
- ○ ....
- ○ ....
- ○ ....
- ○ ....
- ○ ....
- ○ ....
- ○ ....
- ○ ....
- ○ ....
- ○ ....
- ○ ....

TAKE IT TASK BY TASK AND HOUR BY HOUR. USE THESE BLANK PAGES TO MAKE YOUR OWN WINS!

Self CARE

- ○ ....
- ○ ....
- ○ ....
- ○ ....
- ○ ....
- ○ ....
- ○ ....
- ○ ....
- ○ ....
- ○ ....
- ○ ....
- ○ ....
- ○ ....

TAKE IT TASK BY TASK AND HOUR BY HOUR. USE THESE BLANK PAGES TO MAKE YOUR OWN WINS!

Self CARE

- ○ ....
- ○ ....
- ○ ....
- ○ ....
- ○ ....
- ○ ....
- ○ ....
- ○ ....
- ○ ....
- ○ ....
- ○ ....
- ○ ....
- ○ ....

TAKE IT TASK BY TASK AND HOUR BY HOUR. USE THESE BLANK PAGES TO MAKE YOUR OWN WINS!

Self CARE

○ ....
○ ....
○ ....
○ ....
○ ....
○ ....
○ ....
○ ....
○ ....
○ ....
○ ....
○ ....
○ ....

TAKE IT TASK BY TASK AND HOUR BY HOUR. USE THESE BLANK PAGES TO MAKE YOUR OWN WINS!

Self **CARE**

- ○ ....
- ○ ....
- ○ ....
- ○ ....
- ○ ....
- ○ ....
- ○ ....
- ○ ....
- ○ ....
- ○ ....
- ○ ....
- ○ ....
- ○ ....

TAKE IT TASK BY TASK AND HOUR BY HOUR. USE THESE BLANK PAGES TO MAKE YOUR OWN WINS!

Self
CARE

- ○ ....
- ○ ....
- ○ ....
- ○ ....
- ○ ....
- ○ ....
- ○ ....
- ○ ....
- ○ ....
- ○ ....
- ○ ....
- ○ ....

TAKE IT TASK BY TASK AND HOUR BY HOUR. USE THESE BLANK PAGES TO MAKE YOUR OWN WINS!

Self CARE

- ○ ....
- ○ ....
- ○ ....
- ○ ....
- ○ ....
- ○ ....
- ○ ....
- ○ ....
- ○ ....
- ○ ....
- ○ ....
- ○ ....

**TAKE IT TASK BY TASK AND
HOUR BY HOUR. USE THESE
BLANK PAGES TO MAKE
YOUR OWN WINS!**

Self
CARE

○ ....

○ ....

○ ....

○ ....

○ ....

○ ....

○ ....

○ ....

○ ....

○ ....

○ ....

○ ....

TAKE IT TASK BY TASK AND HOUR BY HOUR. USE THESE BLANK PAGES TO MAKE YOUR OWN WINS!

Self CARE

- ○ ....
- ○ ....
- ○ ....
- ○ ....
- ○ ....
- ○ ....
- ○ ....
- ○ ....
- ○ ....
- ○ ....
- ○ ....
- ○ ....
- ○ ....

TAKE IT TASK BY TASK AND HOUR BY HOUR. USE THESE BLANK PAGES TO MAKE YOUR OWN WINS!

Self CARE

- ○ ....
- ○ ....
- ○ ....
- ○ ....
- ○ ....
- ○ ....
- ○ ....
- ○ ....
- ○ ....
- ○ ....
- ○ ....
- ○ ....
- ○ ....

TAKE IT TASK BY TASK AND HOUR BY HOUR. USE THESE BLANK PAGES TO MAKE YOUR OWN WINS!

Self CARE

- ○ ....
- ○ ....
- ○ ....
- ○ ....
- ○ ....
- ○ ....
- ○ ....
- ○ ....
- ○ ....
- ○ ....
- ○ ....
- ○ ....
- ○ ....

TAKE IT TASK BY TASK AND HOUR BY HOUR. USE THESE BLANK PAGES TO MAKE YOUR OWN WINS!

Self
CARE

○ ....
○ ....
○ ....
○ ....
○ ....
○ ....
○ ....
○ ....
○ ....
○ ....
○ ....
○ ....
○ ....

TAKE IT TASK BY TASK AND HOUR BY HOUR. USE THESE BLANK PAGES TO MAKE YOUR OWN WINS!

Self CARE

- ○ ....
- ○ ....
- ○ ....
- ○ ....
- ○ ....
- ○ ....
- ○ ....
- ○ ....
- ○ ....
- ○ ....
- ○ ....
- ○ ....
- ○ ....

TAKE IT TASK BY TASK AND HOUR BY HOUR. USE THESE BLANK PAGES TO MAKE YOUR OWN WINS!

Self CARE

- ⚪ ....
- ⚪ ....
- ⚪ ....
- ⚪ ....
- ⚪ ....
- ⚪ ....
- ⚪ ....
- ⚪ ....
- ⚪ ....
- ⚪ ....
- ⚪ ....
- ⚪ ....

TAKE IT TASK BY TASK AND HOUR BY HOUR. USE THESE BLANK PAGES TO MAKE YOUR OWN WINS!

Self CARE

- ○ ....
- ○ ....
- ○ ....
- ○ ....
- ○ ....
- ○ ....
- ○ ....
- ○ ....
- ○ ....
- ○ ....
- ○ ....
- ○ ....

HAS YOUR CHILD DONE
SOMETHING NEW? WRITE IT
AND DATE IT HERE. CELEBRATE
IT REMEMBER IT FOREVER!

○ ....
○ ....
○ ....
○ ....
○ ....
○ ....
○ ....
○ ....
○ ....
○ ....
○ ....
○ ....

HAS YOUR CHILD DONE SOMETHING NEW? WRITE IT AND DATE IT HERE. CELEBRATE IT REMEMBER IT FOREVER!

○ ....

○ ....

○ ....

○ ....

○ ....

○ ....

○ ....

○ ....

○ ....

○ ....

○ ....

○ ....

HAS YOUR CHILD DONE SOMETHING NEW? WRITE IT AND DATE IT HERE. CELEBRATE IT REMEMBER IT FOREVER!

○ ....

○ ....

○ ....

○ ....

○ ....

○ ....

○ ....

○ ....

○ ....

○ ....

○ ....

○ ....

HAS YOUR CHILD DONE SOMETHING NEW? WRITE IT AND DATE IT HERE. CELEBRATE IT REMEMBER IT FOREVER!

○ ....
○ ....
○ ....
○ ....
○ ....
○ ....
○ ....
○ ....
○ ....
○ ....
○ ....
○ ....
○ ....

HAS YOUR CHILD DONE SOMETHING NEW? WRITE IT AND DATE IT HERE. CELEBRATE IT REMEMBER IT FOREVER!

- ○ ....
- ○ ....
- ○ ....
- ○ ....
- ○ ....
- ○ ....
- ○ ....
- ○ ....
- ○ ....
- ○ ....
- ○ ....
- ○ ....

HAS YOUR CHILD DONE
SOMETHING NEW? WRITE IT
AND DATE IT HERE. CELEBRATE
IT REMEMBER IT FOREVER!

○ ....
○ ....
○ ....
○ ....
○ ....
○ ....
○ ....
○ ....
○ ....
○ ....
○ ....
○ ....
○ ....

HAS YOUR CHILD DONE
SOMETHING NEW? WRITE IT
AND DATE IT HERE. CELEBRATE
IT REMEMBER IT FOREVER!

- ○ ....
- ○ ....
- ○ ....
- ○ ....
- ○ ....
- ○ ....
- ○ ....
- ○ ....
- ○ ....
- ○ ....
- ○ ....
- ○ ....

HAS YOUR CHILD DONE
SOMETHING NEW? WRITE IT
AND DATE IT HERE. CELEBRATE
IT REMEMBER IT FOREVER!

- ⃝ ....
- ⃝ ....
- ⃝ ....
- ⃝ ....
- ⃝ ....
- ⃝ ....
- ⃝ ....
- ⃝ ....
- ⃝ ....
- ⃝ ....
- ⃝ ....
- ⃝ ....
- ⃝ ....

YOUR MEDICAL TEAM
Important Names and Numbers

_____

_____

_____

_____

_____

_____

_____

_____

YOUR MEDICAL TEAM
Important Names and Numbers

YOUR MEDICAL TEAM
Important Names and Numbers

_____

_____

_____

_____

_____

_____

_____

_____

YOUR MEDICAL TEAM
Important Names and Numbers

_____

_____

_____

_____

_____

_____

_____

_____

YOUR MEDICAL TEAM
Important Names and Numbers

_____

_____

_____

_____

_____

_____

_____

_____

YOUR MEDICAL TEAM
Important Names and Numbers

YOUR MEDICAL TEAM
Important Names and Numbers

_____

_____

_____

_____

_____

_____

_____

_____

YOUR MEDICAL TEAM
Important Names and Numbers

_____

_____

_____

_____

_____

_____

_____

_____

END

Printed in Great Britain
by Amazon

ef31eb3c-6514-434b-9627-936cefecaeffR01